D1544328

JET AIRCRAFT

JET AIRCRAFT

MICHAEL HEATLEY

Bison Books

First Published in 1984 by
Bison Books Corp.
17 Sherwood Place
Greenwich, CT 06830

Copyright © 1984 Bison Books Corp.

ISBN 0 86124 177 0

Printed in Hong Kong

CONTENTS

INTRODUCTION

Above: the XP-80A prototype of the Lockheed Shooting Star was one of many pioneer jet aircraft to profit from British aero-engine technology. Although later re-engined, its first flight in January 1944 was completed courtesy of a de Havilland Goblin turbojet.

The development of the jet engine brought the science of aircraft design back to square one. All previous standards of excellence were at once consigned to history as the dividing line was drawn between the ultimate propeller-driven fighters of World War II and the streamlined shapes of the jet age. The Supermarine Spitfire, one of the war's greatest fighters, had suddenly become a museum piece. Although its classic lines had not changed, the possibilities of a new form of propulsion that could be placed inside or outside the airframe demanded a total reappraisal of previously perfected theories and techniques. It was not possible to create a 'jet Spitfire' simply by installing a jet engine; marriages of old airframes and new technology were seldom to be successful.

Although a certain amount of jet engine development had taken place before the outbreak of war, notably in Germany where the turbojet-powered Heinkel He 178 had made its first flight in 1939, it was certain that hostilities accelerated the pace of development on both sides. Greatest results were achieved in Germany, where Heinkel's experiments with jet and rocket power were matched by Messerschmitt with the potent Me 262 jet fighter and the Me 163 *Komet* rocket-powered interceptor. It was only Hitler's personal intervention that prevented the Messerschmitt Me 262, for example, from having a far greater influence on proceedings. It was the Germans, too, who could boast the world's first operational jet bomber in the speedy Arado Ar 234 *Blitz*, but it was only to see limited service, and then mainly in the reconnaissance role.

As World War II drew to a close, it had become obvious that jet propulsion had the potential to revolutionize aircraft design and, through it, the established patterns of aerial warfare. With manufacturing industries operating at high wartime output, the choice was clear – to continue development or to run down to pre-war levels. The United States and Soviet Union followed the former path, seeking the assistance of German experts to advance their cause. Europe was, initially, still recovering from the ravages of war and temporarily *hors de combat*; Britain was content to let others take the lead, while retaining the influential position in jet engine development that had been established as a result of the efforts of Frank Whittle and his team that had started in 1935 with the formation of Power Jets Ltd.

Top left: the trailblazing Heinkel He 178 became the world's first jet aircraft to fly, on 27 August 1939. Top: potentially the most effective fighter of World War II, the Messerschmitt Me 262 was dogged by official disagreement as to its role. Left: the twin-boom configuration of the de Havilland Vampire provided one answer to the problem of jet exhaust for a fuselage-mounted engine.

Although the Gloster E28/39 had not been the first jet aircraft to fly (the Heinkel He 178 having claimed that honor on 27 August 1939), it provided a test bed for Whittle's W1 engine which, after development by Rolls-Royce, became the Welland. This was followed into production by the Derwent, which powered the Meteor, and later the Nene. Designed and constructed in under six months, the Nene was to power a number of important postwar jets, including the Soviet Mikoyan-Gurevich MiG-15.

It was the export of British jet engine expertise that enabled the world's aircraft manufacturers to get their first generation designs off the ground in every sense. The MiG-15 was not the only aircraft to make use of a British-designed engine. France's Dassault Ouragan, Sweden's Saab-29 Tunnan and the US Bell P-59 Airacobra and North American F-86 Sabre all owed a debt to British technology, while many other designs like the Lockheed P-80 Shooting Star, the second American jet to fly (after the P-59), were later to be re-engined with an indigenous power plant after their first flights.

The theme of warfare as a catalyst to development was to be a recurring feature of the jet age, as Soviet-

Right: the world's first production supersonic fighter, the Mikoyan-Gurevich MiG-19 *Farmer,* **in Egyptian service. Below: a Canadian-built North American F-86 Sabre.**

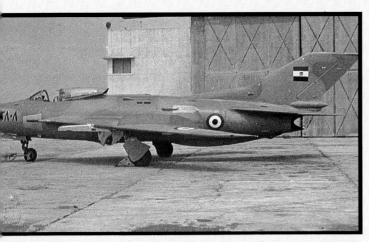

designed MiGs and US Sabres squared up to each other in Korean skies in 1950 and supplied the first clues to the special demands of jet-to-jet combat. Vietnam in the Sixties and Seventies was to see a new, supersonic generation of fighters armed with much more than machine guns usher in the realm of computer dogfighting, while the high-level bombing techniques that had served the Allied bomber force in pounding German cities during World War II were wiped from the warfare rulebook as surface-to-air missiles took their toll of US Boeing B-52 bombers over North Vietnam. The Rockwell B-1B variable-geometry bomber entering service in the Eighties was built to take the stresses of low-level 'under-the-radar' operations.

The Israeli success in the Six Day War of 1967 emphasized the vulnerability of airfields to attack from the air, placing a premium on aircraft that could operate from unprepared strips, roads or even – in the case of the British Aerospace Harrier – take off vertically from a patch of land no bigger than a tennis court. In the Eighties, the Harrier was to compound its versatility by operating from ships, while the deadly French Exocet, launched from Argentine-operated Dassault Super Etendard strikeplanes, emphasized the effectiveness of the latest air-to-surface missiles in the Falklands War of 1982. All these conflicts were observed from the sidelines with interest by the superpowers, seeking indications of the relative strengths and weaknesses of the combat equipment they had, in the main, supplied.

Even by the time of Korea, the swept wing was rapidly becoming the recognized jet planform. As the more powerful piston-engined fighters had approached the speed of sound, shock waves created by the compression of air had interacted to cause buffeting, loss of control and sometimes even complete structural failure. In sweeping back the wing, the shock waves were created *gradually* rather than all at once, keeping them separate and minimizing the risk of turbulence. Once the sound barrier was reached – the Soviet Mikoyan-Gurevich MiG-19 just beating the North American F-100 Super Sabre for the honor of becoming the world's first production supersonic fighter – Mach 2 was not long in coming. (The Mach number was named after Ernst Mach, an influential Nineteenth Century scientist; it expresses the speed of an aircraft in relation to the speed of sound at the altitude at which it is flying.)

From that moment on, the pendulum swung one way, then the other. The missile-shaped Lockheed F-104 Starfighter was first to Mach 2, a matter of months after the MiG-19 had entered service, but the Soviet response to this breakthrough in the sturdy MiG-21 proved more successful in the variety of roles these types were obliged to undertake in the years to come. The next major Soviet advance, the Mach 3 plus MiG-25 *Foxbat*, remained the world's fastest combat type in the Eighties. As with many Soviet aircraft, it first became known to the West as an experimental type, the E-266, which broke world speed records in 1965. It should be remembered, however, that at Mach 3 the *Foxbat* must necessarily fly in a straight line and is therefore of more value as a reconnaissance aircraft than a fighter.

It had taken some time for aircraft armaments to catch up with the revolution in power plant and, later, airframe design that had occurred. The first dogfights between jets in Korea took place with the conventional cannon armament that had gradually superseded the smaller-caliber machine gun during the course of World War II. Indeed, so similar was the initial pattern of warfare in Korean skies to that of the previous conflict that many US world war veterans removed the heavy radar gunsights from their Sabres, preferring to trust their judgment by lining up their guns by means of a chewing-gum mark stuck to the cockpit canopy.

Although the destructive power of the cannon was soon exceeded by the rocket armament of aircraft like the F-86D variant of the North American Sabre and the Lockheed F-94C Starfire, the next major step forward was the advent of the guided air-to-air missile. First of these to enter production in 1954 was the Hughes AIM-4, which brought its considerable capabilities to the USAF's Aerospace Defense Command two years later. Its semi-active radar seeker homed onto energy emitted from the attacking fighter's fire-control radar and reflected by the target. It was followed by a multitude of ever more complex radar-guided weapons that removed the aerial dogfight still further from the World War II pattern as fighters picked each other off from long range.

The other means of missile guidance to come of age in the Fifties was infra-red homing, as pioneered by the AIM-9 Sidewinder. This was attracted to the heat source of the enemy jet's tail pipe and was, in that sense, a true weapon of the jet age, although it paradoxically required the attacking pilot to sit 'on the tail' of his quarry in true Battle of Britain fashion. Infra-red homing lacked the certainty of the radar-guided system, since false targets that emitted heat and/or light (the sun, reflections from roads and lakes) could mislead missiles like the Sidewinder. Nevertheless, the system was admirably simple – a key factor in one-man fighters where the pilot fulfils the weapons-aiming function; it could merely be 'fired and forgotten'. Interceptors of the sixties and after, such as the McDonnell Douglas F-4 Phantom, would typically carry a mix of infra-red and radar-guided weapons to cater for all combat eventualities.

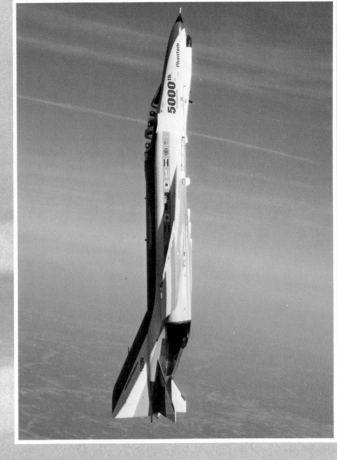

Above: the 5000th McDonnell Douglas F-4 Phantom bears the flags of its many satisfied customer nations. Left: flown by the US Air Force alone, the Boeing B-52 entered service in the mid-fifties and is expected to serve to the end of the century.

On the whole, the jet bomber saw fewer gigantic leaps in performance or changes in design – a fact probably attributable to the varying priority accorded the manned bomber in a postwar period that saw the Intercontinental Ballistic Missile (ICBM) confirmed as the ultimate deterrent to a global aggressor. The mainstay of the US Air Force's bomber fleet in the Sixties and Seventies was the Boeing B-52 Stratofortress which, although impressive in size and payload, proved ever more vulnerable to surface-to-air missile (SAM) attack, as the Vietnam War proved. The Russians opted for a turboprop type, the Tupolev Tu-95 *Bear* with two pure jets, the Tu-16 *Badger* and Myashishchev M-4 *Bison*, supplying limited-range support. Their philosophy was to use the threat of stand-off missiles, delivered from altitude and outside enemy airspace, to counteract the Soviet Union's undoubted technological disadvantage betrayed by the fact that the Tu-95 – like many other Soviet bombers – was based on the outmoded design of the World War II-vintage Boeing B-29.

Britain's futuristic designs, the crescent-wing Handley Page Victor and delta-planform Avro Vulcan, were among the most unusual shapes to appear, but could not rival the eye-catching lines of the North American XB-70 Valkyrie. First flown in 1964 and originally intended as a Mach 3 replacement for the B-52, it was notable only in provoking the design of the Soviet MiG-25 *Foxbat* high-altitude fighter to counter its potential threat. The delta-wing Convair B-58 Hustler had gained the distinction of becoming the world's first production supersonic bomber, serving with the USAF from 1959, but did not remain operational beyond the Sixties due to its high cost of operation. Only the Dassault Mirage IV, a scaled-up version of the French designer's fighter series, was to prove a total success in the first-generation supersonic bomber stakes.

Faster speeds inevitably meant greater risks – particularly when the aircraft concerned were breaking new ground. The British Martin-Baker company was in the forefront of the development of the ejection seat, the first airborne tests of which took place in 1946. Rockets propelled the pilot from his aircraft on a detachable seat, enabling him to descend safely by parachute. The ejection seat quickly became standard equipment in all jet fighters although some ideas, like the 'downward ejection' of the Lockheed F-104 Starfighter, were highly unconventional.

The system's ultimate development was the 'zero-zero' ejection seat that could shoot a pilot to safety from ground level (zero altitude) at zero speed, for example on aborted take-off from an aircraft carrier. Escape capsules enjoyed a period of popularity, particularly in the design of such multi-crew types as the Convair B-58 Hustler supersonic bomber and the General Dynamics F-111, both unconventional designs of their day in other respects. The inevitable complexity of this arrangement found little favor

Top and right: the predatory shape of Britain's Avro Vulcan. Above: the mighty Soviet Tupolev Tu-95 *Bear*. Below right: Convair's B-58 Hustler.

elsewhere, however, and multiple ejection seats were more usual.

Developments in jet aircraft design by the Western powers seemed to slow down in the post 'Cold War' period as a direct result of increasing emphasis on missiles as the most effective method of offense/defense, and the imposition of budget restrictions. The increasing expense of developing new high-performance combat types led to such multi-national collaborations as the Panavia Tornado – which, in the Eighties, forms the backbone of the air forces of Britain, Germany and Italy in its attack and interceptor variants – the Anglo-French SEPECAT Jaguar strike/trainer, and the Anglo-American Harrier development, the McDonnell Douglas AV-8B. The success of such shared-risk ventures makes it almost certain that there will be fewer shapes in the sky in the future as basically similar aircraft fulfil multiple roles.

A major postwar innovation that shrank the world map in aviation terms was in-flight refueling. Two systems were initially proposed, the 'flying boom' employed by the USAF's KC-135 tanker version of the civil Boeing 707 jetliner, and the 'probe and drogue' method, pioneered in Britain, that became the

accepted standard in the West. This technique involves trailing a hose with a drogue (funnel-shaped) attachment into which the receiving aircraft maneuvers its flight refueling probe. The tactical options this concept presents are numerous, enabling strike aircraft to fly deep-penetration missions into enemy territory, fighters to extend their endurance on patrol and all types to increase their ferry range.

Several obsolescent bomber types have enjoyed new leases of life as flight refueling tankers, including the British Valiant, Victor and Vulcan and the Soviet Tu-16 *Badger* and M-4 *Bison.* As bombers have remained longer in service, however, airliners such as the Lockheed TriStar have provided the basis for the second generation of tankers entering service in the Eighties. Some modern combat jets such as the Panavia Tornado can act as their own tankers, practicing 'buddy' refueling to extend range. Flight refueling has considerably blurred the distinction between tactical (short-range) and strategic (inter-continental-range) types, permitting aircraft with a known limited range to present a new threat to distant targets.

While the US took a breather in the wake of the disastrous involvement in Vietnam and with a proven backbone of modern combat types such as the McDonnell Douglas F-4 Phantom and the swing-wing General Dynamics F-111, Britain was still struggling to reverse the decade and a half of stagnation that had followed the 1957 White Paper that foresaw no role for manned aircraft in future conflicts. The Soviet Union, meanwhile, made use of the opportunity to catch up. Not being as subject to the restrictions on defense spending found in the West, the USSR was in a position not only to consolidate but also make the running in jet aircraft design for perhaps the first time. Although it entered service in 1969, the Sukhoi Su-15 was a missile-armed interceptor that matched the best in the West and was still in the air defense front line 15 years later. The Sukhoi bureau followed this with the Su-24 *Fencer,* a variable-geometry multi-role type that simultaneously overhauled the General Dynamics F-111 while proving a match for the latest American offering, the US Navy's Grumman F-14 Tomcat.

The high-speed, high altitude MiG-25 *Foxbat* was another Soviet design of the Sixties that was to remain unchallenged in the Seventies, a fact underlined when a number of these aircraft overflew Israel in 1971 at speeds and altitudes well beyond the home country's F-4 Phantom interceptors. It wasn't until the advent of the identically configured McDonnell Douglas F-15 Eagle that the West could boast anything remotely comparable.

In the attack and bombing fields, too, the Soviet design bureaux caught up with and then overhauled their rivals. The Mikoyan-Gurevich MiG-23 and MiG-27 fighter and attack types paralleled the McDonnell Douglas F-4, while the strategic capa-

Above: the SEPECAT Jaguar started life as a trainer, but was also produced as an attack aircraft. Above right: the McDonnell Douglas F-4 Phantom shared the interception and attack roles. Right: tankbusting is the specialized task of the Fairchild A-10 Thunderbolt II. Below right: the sleek shape of the McDonnell Douglas F-15 Eagle air superiority fighter.

bility of the Tupolev Tu-26 *Backfire* was allied to Mach 2 performance. The boot was now on the other foot; while the Soviets had patiently been forced to update and refurbish old equipment, they now boasted a significant new bomber while the once-proud Strategic Air Command of the USAF was faced with the probability of flying the venerable B-52 into the next century.

Ever since the appearance of the German V2 rocket in World War II, it had been widely assumed that the future of warfare would be in the shape of missiles. The appearance of *Backfire,* however, forced the US to take another look at an air defense system that in the late Seventies depended on a mixture of some 300 decidedly elderly F-101 Voodoo, F-106 Delta Dart and F-4 Phantom interceptors. At the same time, the continuing eruption of conventional conflicts (particularly in the Middle East) emphasized the need for aircraft that can offer an effective non-nuclear response. The appearance of the Fairchild A-10 Thunderbolt II tankbuster was clearly developed with a conventional confrontation in Europe between NATO and the Soviet bloc in mind, and as a result of the imbalance between Soviet and NATO armor.

Having single-handedly led the world in the field of vertical take-off, Britain had let her lead slip away by the Eighties. Although the revolutionary Hawker Siddeley (British Aerospace) Harrier proved a world-beating design, there was little sign of official backing for further development. With the cancellation of the P1154 Mach 2 VTOL project in the mid-Sixties, the

way was clear for the United States – in the shape of the McDonnell Douglas Corporation – to explore the concept further with the AV-8B 'Advanced Harrier' in the Eighties.

Strangely, the Soviet Union had proved unable to challenge Western supremacy in the VTOL field in the intervening period. The Yakovlev Yak-36 *Forger*, their key challenger, lacked the range and performance to approach the Harrier. Despite the flight deck of Soviet *Kiev* class vessels on which it is deployed, the Yak-36 cannot take off on a short run; it can only take off vertically, a fact that limits its payload. For despite the revolutionary vertical take-off concept, the Harrier usually uses a short take-off run (when available) to increase its warload.

By the Seventies, the turbofan had eclipsed the pure jet as the preferred power plant for Western warplanes on the grounds of economy. The turbojet sucks air into its compressor, squeezes it into a dense, oxygen-rich mixture and combines it with kerosene before ignition. It is the 'equal and opposite reaction' of Newtonian physics that provides the thrust. With the turbofan, however, most of the air intake by-passes the combustion chamber, providing a larger volume of air that makes up for the slower speed at which the airflow leaves the engine.

The fuel saved by 'scaling down' the combustion mechanism provides bombers like the Tu-26 *Backfire* with greater range and fighters like the F-14 Tomcat with greater endurance. The turboprop had long offered fuel economy, but at speeds greater than 450mph problems were often encountered with propeller tips approaching the speed of sound. Now the turbofan combined turboprop economy with turbojet speed.

The main jet combat types of the world's air forces can be divided into three categories; fighters, bombers and attack aircraft. Fighters, inevitably, push the frontiers of flight ever onward and upward; bombers are faced with a bewildering array of defensive missiles and related weapons through which they must press home their assault; while attack aircraft, for so long the poor relation in air warfare, have in the Eighties come to be regarded as operating in a specialist field requiring purpose-built designs to hit ground targets with precision.

In spite of the high hopes placed on nuclear missiles as a global deterrent to ensure world peace, the possibility of conventional warfare somewhere in the world is constantly with us. For as long as the future of manned flight is assured, there is a place for the jet aircraft – and, if the example of the Hawker Hunter, first flown in 1951 and still in active service in the Lebanon in 1983, is any indication, many of the aircraft in this book will still be important in the next century.

Right: a near-unique vertical take-off and landing capability made the British Aerospace Harrier a world-beater. A Sea Harrier is pictured.

FIGHTERS

In spite of the almost limitless possibilities suggested by jet propulsion, jet fighters had little effect on the course of World War II. Of the two opposing types to see action for a significant period, the Luftwaffe's Messerschmitt Me 262 was far superior in design and performance to the RAF's Gloster Meteor, despite their similarities in engines and armament. The German design was also suitable for fighter-bomber operations – a fact that was to play a significant part in its downfall, since Hitler insisted that aircraft on the production line be completed as fighter-bombers despite an Allied bombing campaign then striking at the heart of the Reich that suggested the fighter should be given priority.

This misguided decision, taken at the very highest level, not only reduced numbers of fighters available, but delayed their introduction to service. The other German jet fighter to reach operational status was the comparatively crude Heinkel He 162 *Volksjäger*, a type intended for operation by untrained youth volunteers. Despite having been first off the mark with the He 178 as war loomed in 1939, Ernst Heinkel had encountered official indifference to his researches, as well as splitting his options by investigating rocket power with a parallel project, the He 176.

Although some 120mph inferior to the Messerschmitt Me 262, the Gloster Meteor was never made to suffer for this since Meteor-Messerschmitt combat was never to take place. Instead, the Meteor was introduced to service in 1944 and immediately made its mark against the V1 flying bombs then being launched from the continent, destroying them both by means of its four-cannon armament and by unbalancing the rocket's gyroscopically-controlled flight by wing-tipping it out of control. Ironically, the V1 was also jet-propelled, but its pulse jet was too unreliable for manned aircraft.

At the war's end, the United States and Soviet Union scrambled to utilize the techniques and technicians of the vanquished nation. The United Kingdom, meanwhile, consolidated her lead in jet-engine technology simply by switching from the bulky and complex centrifugal-flow concept to the simpler and more compact axial-flow engines. Sadly, the late Forties and early Fifties saw her concede preeminence in the field of jet fighter design to the United States and Soviet Union – both of whose early fighters, ironically, were initially built around license-manufactured versions of British engines.

The first barrier to higher speeds was not the sound barrier itself but the straight-wing planform adopted by both the Meteor and its US counterpart, the Lockheed P-80 Shooting Star. The swept wing of the Me 262 showed the way ahead and, while Lockheed continued the F-80 line with the F-94 Starfire allweather interceptor, and Republic unveiled the highly conventional straight-wing F-84 Thunderjet, North American – now released from Mustang production – took a fresh look at the problem. The result was the swept-wing F-86 Sabre, which made its first flight in October 1947 (powered by the Wright J65 version of the Armstrong Siddeley Sapphire engine) and entered US Air Force service in 1949.

Previous pages: first flown in 1954, the pencil-thin Lockheed F-104 Starfighter took the jet fighter to Mach 2 and beyond. Above: switching from piston-engined fighters to jets was a problem the two-seat Messerschmitt Me 262B-1a trainer was intended to solve. Below: an all-weather variant of the North American Sabre, the F-86K, in Norwegian service.

The Soviet Union had reached the same conclusion, eventually rejecting the straight-wing designs proffered by the Yakovlev bureau in favor of Mikoyan's MiG-15, first flown 12 weeks after the F-86 and code-named *Fagot* by NATO. With its gaping nose engine intake and all-swept flying surfaces, it was superficially quite similar to its US rival, a fin-mounted tailplane providing the easiest distinguishing feature. The types' relative merits were soon to be revealed, however, in the harsh light of warfare when the outbreak of hostilities in Korea in 1950 saw the United Nations and the Communist bloc race to the aid of South and North respectively.

With little more than five years having elapsed since World War II, it was inevitable that the pattern of dogfighting should at first be similar – indeed, the US pilots' combat experience resulted in a number of piston-and-jet aces (pilots who shot down five or more enemy aircraft in each conflict). Although it was a Lockheed P-80 that claimed the first MiG victim in jet-to-jet combat, it was the Sabre that was to prove the master of Korean skies. It had a 10mph advantage in speed over the Russian at sea level, while the MiG's superior agility, rate of climb and turning circle at altitudes over 25,000 feet saw North Korean pilots seek sanctuary in higher levels of operation. The secondment of Soviet pilots could not alter the course of events, however, and when the F-86F arrived at the front line with its more efficient wing improving high-altitude performance, a kill ratio of the order of 9:1 in the Sabre's favor had already been established. At the Korean Armistice in mid-1953, a score of 792 downed MiGs for the loss of 104 Sabres of all marks told its own story.

The significance of the F-86D 'Sabre Dog', introduced to service in 1953, stemmed both from its visual trademark radar scanner housed in a 'bullet' nose fairing and its armament of 24 2.75-inch rockets,

Above: de Havilland's Sea Vixen shipboard fighter. Below: the Gloster Javelin brought an all-weather capability to the Royal Air Force. Bottom: undoubtedly the most successful British jet fighter of all time, the BAC Lightning served into the eighties.

Top: McDonnell's contribution to the US Century Series of fighters was the F-101 Voodoo. Above: a Convair F-102 Delta Dagger returns from a sortie.

vice in 1951, initially powered by a license-built de Havilland Ghost turbojet.

The French, too, were entering the jet age, despite the added handicap of having to rebuild their aircraft industry. Noted pre-war designer Marcel Bloch, released from captivity, changed his name to Dassault and came up with the Ouragan (Hurricane). Power-plant difficulties were overcome by license-manu-facture of the Rolls-Royce Nene and, with 30 degrees of wing sweep, the Ouragan became the Mystère. When re-engined with the SNECMA Atar, the first French turbojet, this became the first European aircraft to break the sound barrier. Continuing jet fighter development by Dassault was to result in the world-beating Mirage series of fighters, bombers and attack aircraft in the Sixties.

Back in Britain at the start of the Fifties, the twin-boom de Havilland Vampire, of which over 3000 examples were built, continued to serve with the Royal Air Force and the air arms of several other countries. The Vampire had flown for the first time in 1943, entering RAF service nearly three years later, but its design was far from innovatory, its nose section owing much to the 'wooden wonder' Mosquito bomber. De Havilland was later to duplicate the twin-boom configuration with the Sea Vixen shipboard all-weather fighter, powered by two Rolls-Royce Avon turbojets, that entered service with the Fleet Air Arm in the mid-Fifties.

In 1951, a trio of modern-looking land-based fighters took to the air for the first time – the Hawker Hunter, Supermarine Scimitar and Supermarine Swift. The last-named became the RAF's first swept-wing fighter two years later, but was to survive barely that time in front-line service.

The Scimitar replaced the straight-wing Attacker in Fleet Air Arm service from 1958, but it was the Hunter that was to prove its pedigree with a long career. Designed by Hurricane architect Sydney Camm, it was a sturdy and reliable aircraft that excelled in the ground-attack role where its subsonic performance was of secondary importance. The Gloster Javelin, too, was emphatically subsonic, despite its much-vaunted all-weather capability, and it was not until the arrival of the English Electric (later BAC) Lightning, a true Mach 2 interceptor designed by W E W 'Teddy' Petter, that the RAF would be able to employ an indigenously designed and built supersonic fighter.

The speed of development was considerably faster in the United States, where the Century Series of fighters – a name that reflected both their designations and their supersonic performance – was progressing from drawing-board to runway. All utilized a new form of thrust augmentation known as afterburning or reheat. This involved injecting fuel into the exhaust gases of the engine to provide extra thrust for little extra weight. Used mainly for take-off or combat chase, the technique was thenceforth widely used.

carried in a retractable ventral tray and fireable in bursts of 6 or 12. Hailed as the world's first swept-wing all-weather fighter, the F-86D could fly what was known as a 'collision-course' combat pattern, delivering its warload with the aid of its APG-37 radar, rather than maneuvering behind its adversary in the conventional 'chase' dogfight. Rockets, too, were significant, since the Sabre's thin wing had hitherto limited the type's armament-carrying poten-tial to six nose-mounted machine guns.

In Europe, meanwhile, the Swedes had taken advantage of their wartime neutrality to press forward with jet fighter development. Although they had been experimenting with turbojets prior to the outbreak of World War II, they elected to produce their first jet fighter by re-engining the Model 21A, a piston-engined, pusher-configured monoplane, with a British turbojet, the Goblin. The lessons learned with the resulting Model 21-R were swiftly put into practice with the design of the Saab-29 Tunnan (Barrel), a short, stubby and unattractive type that nevertheless earned the distinction of becoming Europe's first operational swept-wing fighter when it entered ser-

As its name suggested, the North American F-100 Super Sabre started life as a development of the F-86, but rapidly built a reputation in its own right once a series of development problems relating to instability at high speeds had been overcome. Despite these, it was the first aircraft to pass Mach 1 in level flight. The F-100 was unusual in having no flaps, as ailerons were fitted inboard where flaps would normally be found. The 'Hun', as it was affectionately known to its pilots, survived to serve in Vietnam, where the two-seat F-100F combat trainer was pressed into service against surface-to-air missile sites in so-called 'Wild Weasel' operations.

The McDonnell F-101 Voodoo had originally been intended as a long-range escort fighter for US heavy bombers, but turned out instead to be a long-serving if unspectacular supersonic interceptor fighter. It remained a vital link in the NORAD (North American Air Defense Command) defense chain for many years after its introduction to service in the late Fifties with the US and, later, Canadian Air Forces.

Unlike the Voodoo, the Convair F-102 Delta Dagger *was* conceived as a supersonic interceptor, but its introduction to service was considerably delayed by shortcomings in speed and ceiling. It was only through the concept of 'area ruling' – dictating that the fuselage be 'waisted' to bulge like a Coke bottle in plan view at nose and tail – that the sound barrier was finally attained. The F-102B (later F-106) Delta Dart development proved more successful and had a genuine Mach 2 performance, although the attendant delays in the program resulted in the USAF taking delivery of only some 35 percent of the original order. Nevertheless, the missile-armed F-106 remained a front-line interceptor for over two decades before giving way to the McDonnell Douglas F-15 Eagle.

First of the USAF's Mach 2 fighters to fly was the Lockheed F-104 Starfighter, created by Clarence 'Kelly' Johnson. He based the design on the comments of combat pilots with Korean War combat experience, building it around the newly-developed General Electric J79 turbojet that went on to power the Phantom and many other exceptional warplanes. Dubbed the 'manned missile', the minimum-wing F-104 made its maiden flight in 1954 – but development was long and costly and the US Air Force was less than keen on re-ordering a type that had taken

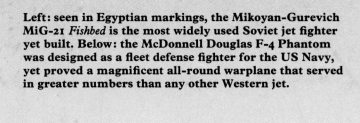

four years to place into service. Then a consortium of NATO air arms, among them West Germany, Holland and Italy as well as Japan, rescued the project by selecting the type as their standard multi-role fighter for the Sixties.

Built under license in several countries, the F-104G (the suffix letter indicating Germany) was fitted with a fire-control radar and an inertial navigation system, but quickly ran into trouble despite such sophistication. The type, after all, had been intended for the high-altitude interception role – but pressed into service at low levels, without hangar protection from the elements and flown by inexperienced pilots, the loss rate rapidly rose to a mid-Sixties peak of one every ten days. Little wonder, then, that the F-104G quickly became known as the Widowmaker in German service. The problems were eventually ironed out, although the final Starfighter variant, the F-104S for Italy and Turkey, wisely reverted to the type's original interceptor role.

Meanwhile, the prolific and influential Mikoyan-Gurevich design bureau had not been idle in preparing Iron-Curtain counterparts to the impressive array of US fighters detailed above. The MiG-17 *Fresco* development of the MiG-15 had taken the first-generation design as far as it would go and the MiG-19, although superficially similar, was in fact completely new. Its slimmer fuselage betrayed the fact that it was built around the first sizeable Soviet-built axial-flow turbojet, the Lyulka AL-5, rather than its predecessors' bulkier centrifugal-flow power plants. In the event, development hitches led to the AL-5's replacement by a pair of Tumansky RD-9 turbojets, beginning a long association between engine and airframe manufacturers. The MiG-19, code-named *Farmer* by NATO, had true supersonic performance in level flight and was therefore a contemporary of the US F-100. It was also a pilot's airplane and a delight to fly – so much so that the usual UTI-suffix two-seat training version was never placed in production, pilots graduating from the smaller MiG trainers to the new type with confidence.

The MiG-19 was swiftly to be overtaken, however, by Mikoyan's next creation, the MiG-21, and production was switched from the Soviet Union to Czechoslovakia in 1958 for its last three years. Nevertheless, the type proved of continued significance by providing the basis for Chinese air power in the Sixties and Seventies in an unlicensed copy version, the Shenyang J-6 *Fantan*. It retained the powerful three-cannon armament that made the MiG-19 a particularly potent threat, and over 10,000 were reckoned to have been built by the Eighties, when limited production continued. Export orders were received from Pakistan, Tanzania, Bangladesh, Kampuchea and Vietnam. A Mach 1.35 redesign with wing-root air intakes and a pointed nose was also developed and exported to Pakistan in the late Seventies as the Nanzhang Q-5 attack fighter (NATO designation *Fantan-A*).

The British aircraft industry had faced the Sixties in the knowledge that a 1957 defense review White Paper had foreseen air defense switching from manned aircraft to missiles. The P1 experimental supersonic project that was later to become the Lightning was allowed to proceed, but no further manned fighter projects were to be authorized. It was as well, then, that the Lightning proved to be one of the great British success stories of the postwar era, emerging as an all-weather interceptor fighter with a top speed of Mach 2.

Development was necessarily slow, given the innovative nature of the design and the ground that the British aircraft industry had to make up. Although the Lightning was cleared for RAF service in 1960, it took four more years for the F Mark 3 to enter service with more fuel, more powerful Rolls-Royce Avon engines and collision-course fire control for the two Red Top or Firestreak air-to-air missiles tucked snugly under the leading edge of the razor-sharp, abbreviated wing. Although this armament, even when combined with the two 30mm Aden cannon of later versions, failed to approach the firepower of the McDonnell Douglas F-4 Phantom, the RAF's other interceptor in the Seventies, the fast-climbing Lightning enjoyed a decade and a half of effective service.

Elsewhere in Europe, jet fighter design had been actively encouraged, and the results were, in many cases, spectacular to behold. Saab had followed up the ungainly Tunnan with the Hunter-like Lansen (Lance), powered by the Hunter's Rolls-Royce Avon engine with a Swedish-developed afterburner adding a punch. This was to be Saab's last 'conventional' fighter design, since the Draken and, later, Viggen that followed the Lansen off the production lines were striking in appearance indeed.

Above: most spectacular but least successful variation on Marcel Dassault's Mirage theme was the vertical take-off III-V. Below: when re-engined with the Phantom's General Electric J79 engine and boasting 'canard' foreplanes for maneuverability, the Mirage became the Israel Aircraft Industries Kfir-C2.

The Draken first flew in 1955, although its double-delta wing had already been the subject of extensive testing. The efficiency of the unusual wing planform was swiftly apparent when, during routine pre-service evaluation, the Draken exceeded Mach 2. This was all the more remarkable when it is remembered that the Draken's power plant was an uprated version of the same Avon engine that had powered the (subsonic) Lansen; the English Electric Lightning was to need two Avons to achieve a similar performance. Entering service with the Swedish Flygvapnet in 1960, the Draken carried four Sidewinder air-to-air missiles and two Aden cannon. The type was constantly updated with fire-control radar and later a Hughes weapons system, and attracted export orders from Denmark and Finland that kept the production lines open into the Seventies.

The Viggen, in many ways the Draken's successor,

series continued to be developed for another quarter-century in various forms. The Mirage III, a tailless delta-wing single-seater, proved the mainstay, and demonstrated its flexibility by being built in fighter-bomber, ground attack and interceptor versions. The Mirage had originated as a private venture following an official requirement for a rocket-and-jet powered interceptor (the rocket was rarely used, and was deleted in later export examples). Swift backing from the Armée de l'Air, which ordered ten aircraft only six months after the Mirage's first flight in November 1956, saw the project off to a promising start, and the

matched its predecessor's unusual shape by employing a delta with foreplanes – shoulder-mounted 'canard' flying surfaces with flaps above the engine intakes. The short take-off capability the configuration conferred would allow the Viggen to fly from ice, snow, fields or roads in time of war. Powered by a Swedish-built Pratt & Whitney JT8D turbofan, the single-seat Viggen emulated the Draken's Mach 2 performance, but boasted in addition a staggeringly complex, computerized weapons system that enabled it to carry out attack missions as effectively as a two-man-crewed aircraft. Reconnaissance and interceptor Viggens followed the initial AJ37 into service in the mid-Seventies and are expected to provide the backbone of Sweden's air defense until the arrival of the SAAB 2110/JAS39 in the Nineties.

The French, meanwhile, had developed their own effective family of fighters in the Dassault Mirage series. After claiming the honor of being the first European aircraft to exceed Mach 2 in 1958, the

first production examples were delivered in 1960. Since then, over a dozen countries have ordered the type, while a simplified ground-attack variant, the Mirage 5, found favor with a number of Third World countries. Re-engined with a higher-rated SNECMA Atar turbojet, this became the Mirage 50 in the late Seventies.

Further developments of the Mirage included the unsuccessful vertical take-off Mirage III-V, the variable-geometry Mirage G and the larger Mirage IV supersonic bomber. Common components and design features enabled these variants to be constructed at relatively low cost. The Mirage III's successor as an interceptor in French service was the Mirage F1, also powered by a SNECMA Atar turbojet, but with the addition of conventional horizontal tail surfaces. It boasted a 10 percent higher maximum speed (Mach 2.2), three times the endurance and twice the range of its predecessor, together with improved take-off and general handling characteristics.

Meanwhile, the Mirage III was gaining a new lease of life in the Middle East, where Israel Aircraft Industries evolved their own development of the type with foreplanes and the General Electric J79 engine of the Phantom as the IAI Kfir-C2. This renaissance was completed when, to bring the tale full circle, the Mirage 2000 was selected as the primary combat aircraft of the French Armée de l'Air from the mid-Eighties. Its reversion to the delta-wing of the Mirage III/5 series was perhaps surprising after the F1's departure from tradition, but in concluding that the planform offered the best compromise between simplicity, weight, maneuverability and high-speed

handling, the researchers pinpointed Marcel Dassault's farsightedness in the Fifties. With a SNECMA M53 afterburning turbofan engine, the Mirage 2000 is scheduled to enter service in the mid-Eighties and carry the Mirage name into the next century. A twin turbofan multi-role Super Mirage 4000 was also under development.

Numerically the most successful Western jet fighter ever, the McDonnell Douglas F-4 Phantom II remains one of the most versatile and adaptable combat types in the early Eighties, a quarter-century after its first flight. Winning an initial US Navy order for 375 aircraft, the two-seat Phantom was developed into a multi-mission fighter-bomber that saw service with the USAF and the air arms of nearly a dozen other countries – over 20 percent of Phantom production was for export. In the air defense role, it can carry a mix of four infra-red Sidewinder and a similar number of radar-homing Sparrow missiles, while cannon, rockets and a 16,000 pound bomb-load are among its options in the attack configuration. Over 5000 Phantoms were built and, while it is far from the world's most graceful fighter, its twin General Electric J79 afterburning turbojets power it to a maximum speed at altitude of Mach 2.17. Over a dozen speed, time-to-height and altitude records have fallen to the Phantom since its maiden flight in 1958, confirming the F-4 as one of the outstanding combat aircraft of the jet age.

The Mikoyan-Gurevich MiG-21 is the only fighter to challenge the Phantom as the world's most widely used jet fighter. Like the F-104 Starfighter, its roots were in the combat experiences of the Korean War, where the MiG-15's performance had not been enough to gain it mastery of the skies. The MiG-21 Fishbed took shape in the two years following Korea, and reflected the Soviet pilots' desire for a simple, maneuverable clear-weather interceptor. Its lightness and simple tailed-delta design made it the cheapest Mach 2 fighter ever developed. Once the MiG-21F had entered service in late 1959, the type underwent the traditional Soviet program of continuous im-

provement – the first fruit of which was seen in 1961 with the appearance of the PF-suffix all-weather interceptor with a small radar in the nose intake cone. Powered by a single Tumansky afterburning turbo-jet, the MiG-21 supplemented its twin-barrel cannon armament with four *Atoll* air-to-air missiles, but suffered the handicap common among Soviet fighter designs of a limited range and endurance due to insufficient fuel reserves.

The other Soviet design bureau to be developing fighters parallel to the US Century Series in the Fifties was that of Pavel Sukhoi. The Su-7 and Su-9 both made their first public appearance in 1956 at the Tushino Aviation Day: the Su-7, code-named *Fitter*, by the West, was a swept-wing ground attack type, while the Su-9 *Fishpot* was an all-weather interceptor with a delta wing but otherwise similar in configuration to its sister design. But while the Su-7 (described elsewhere) was widely exported to Soviet bloc and sympathetic countries alike, the Su-9 and its development the Su-11 remained in Soviet service alone.

If the Su-9/11 series could be likened to a less powerful version of the RAF's Lightning, then the Su-15 *Flagon* took its wing, tail, undercarriage and armament and mated it to a larger body with twin Tumansky turbojets to provide a second-generation supersonic interceptor. Equipped with two *Anab* air-to-air missiles, one radar-homing and the other infra-red homing, *Flagon* carries no built-in gun armament. The type is believed to have been responsible for the destruction of the Korean Air Lines Boeing 747 that strayed into Soviet airspace in 1983.

The Seventies saw a new rash of fighters from both

Below: although not strictly a fighter, British Aerospace's Hawk is typical of many jet trainers in having a secondary arms-carrying capability; two AIM-9L Sidewinder air-to-air missiles equip it for air defense.

sides of the Iron Curtain, many making use of a variable-geometry (or swing) wing. The low-speed handling characteristics and lengthy landing runs of supersonic fighters had long been a cause for concern; types like the Lockheed F-104 and English Electric Lightning, for example, had displayed less than tolerant tendencies when flying outside the fast-and-high regime in which they had been designed to operate most efficiently. The VG planform offered a way around this; by offering a near-straight wing for landing, maximum lift and minimum landing roll could be achieved; full wing sweepback transformed the aircraft into a streamlined, high-speed fighter, while economy cruise with the wing in an intermediate position conserved fuel and thereby extended range and/or endurance. The penalties to be paid for this 'perfect solution', however, were in the weight and complexity of the mechanism needed to effect wing sweep in flight.

The aircraft that single-handedly brought variable geometry to the front line (though not without some teething troubles along the way) was the General Dynamics F-111. Originally commissioned to fulfil the TFX (Tactical Fighter, Experimental) requirement for a fleet fighter to replace the US Navy's F-4 Phantoms while doubling as an Air Force fighter-bomber in the mold of the F-105 Thunderchief, the F-111 first flew in late 1964. The first requirement soon proved beyond its capabilities; as drag and low maneuverability were compensated for by increased fuel load, the type began to look overfed for an air defense fighter, and an order for 231 F-111Bs for the US Navy was cancelled. After an eventful flight-test

program, the F-111 was sent to South-East Asia for operational trials early in 1968, but the loss of three of the six aircraft in four weeks led to more modifications, notably to the engine air inlets.

Ultimate production version of the F-111 was the F-111F; with its more powerful Pratt & Whitney TF30 turbofans adding much-needed extra thrust, it finally fulfilled the type's design potential, but had become so expensive by its introduction in the mid-Seventies that the US Air Force was limited to purchasing only around 100 of them. A strategic bombing variant, the FB-111, was also restricted in production, in this case to under 100 aircraft.

Despite the problems encountered by General Dynamics in bringing the F-111 design to fruition, by the end of the Seventies both East and West boasted a number of variable-geometry types in front-line service. Although rather smaller than the US machine, the Soviet MiG-23 *Flogger* represented their biggest step forward in terms of air superiority at low-to-medium altitudes since the MiG-21. Comparable to the Saab Viggen in size, the MiG-23 underwent considerable revision – mainly in the tail and wing leading edge regions – as stability problems were overcome in the late Sixties/early Seventies. The resulting MiG-23S carried pairs of *Apex* and *Aphid* air-to-air missiles to supplement its twin-barrel cannon in the air superiority role. A secondary strike capability was also foreseen for the MiG-23 but the development of the MiG-27 attack variant eventually took on an identity of its own; this is described elsewhere. The MiG-23 was exported to all Warsaw Pact air forces except that of Romania.

The United Kingdom had been left all but bereft of air defense in the Sixties, the number of RAF fighter squadrons having been reduced from 55 to five in the decade following the infamous 1957 defense review. Purchases of the McDonnell Douglas F-4 Phantom helped the Lightning shore up the creaking defenses, but it was not until the advent of the variable-geometry Panavia Tornado ADV (Air Defense Variant), designated Tornado F Mark 2 in RAF service, in the mid-Eighties that the damage could be considered undone. This variant of the Tornado (described more fully in the attack section) carries AIM-9L Super Sidewinder and Sky Flash missiles, as well as sporting a 27mm cannon for dogfighting.

Further assistance will be provided by the British Aerospace Hawk, the RAF's standard intermediate flying and weapons trainer, which can carry Sidewinder missiles for airfield defense. The Hawk replaced the Folland Gnat (originally an Mach 0.98 lightweight fighter) in the training role. Although never armed in RAF service, the Gnat flew as a fighter with the air forces of Finland and India, the last-named building its own Gnat development named Ajeet (Invincible) in the Seventies and Eighties. Other widely-used jet trainers to double in an offensive role included the Czech Aero L-39 Albatros and the Italian Aermacchi MB 339, while the Dassault/Breguet/Dornier Alpha Jet began to replace the venerable Potez Magister, Dassault Mystère and other types in the late Seventies.

It would be strictly inaccurate to include the Northrop F-5 Freedom Fighter in this list since the T-38 Talon trainer from which it emerged had itself been schemed as a lightweight fighter, the N-156, in the mid-Fifties. After many years' service with foreign air arms, the F-5 was eventually adopted by the USAF in 1973 to simulate Soviet aircraft during exercises – 12 years after the Talon had been accepted as the world's first supersonic basic trainer.

Having been developed to counter the threat of the US Mach 3 XB-70 Valkyrie bomber, the MiG-25 Foxbat was intended for operation at altitudes of up to 80,000 feet at speeds exceeding Mach 3. When the XB-70 was cancelled, the Foxbat's role was redefined to include high-altitude reconnaissance while retaining its armament of four air-to-air missiles. Although examination of a defector's MiG-25 in Japan in 1976 showed avionics and fire control system to be rudimentary in design, the speed of Foxbat (estimated at Mach 3.2, with a 'never exceed' of Mach 2.8 with external stores) remained unequalled in the mid-Eighties, some twenty years after the type's first world speed records.

The US Air Force added two significant new single-seat fixed-wing fighter types to its inventory in the Seventies: the McDonnell Douglas F-15 Eagle and the diminutive General Dynamics F-16 Fighting Falcon. The two were in many respects dissimilar – the F-15 a fully-automated, twin-turbofan giant with more offensive/defensive electronics than any previous combat aircraft, the F-16 a nimble tactical lightweight fighter designed to present a difficult target.

The F-15 was developed in response to the MiG-25 Foxbat, the world's fastest operation fighter. It was remarkably similar in configuration to its rival, with twin vertical tail surfaces, shoulder-mounted wing and gaping air intakes for its twin engines, while its maximum speed of Mach 2.5, though inferior, was not incomparable. Besides this, the Eagle's cockpit and avionics display and low-speed maneuverability were considerably superior to that of Foxbat.

Although smaller and less complex, the F-16 could prove equally successful. It was created quickly in the early Seventies around just one of the Pratt & Whitney F100 turbofans that powered the F-15 – but was far more than half the aircraft. The engine was fed by a large air intake beneath the forward fuselage that limited the F-16's maximum speed to Mach 1.8, but

Above left: the versatile, variable-geometry Panavia
Tornado. Above: Mikoyan-Gurevich's MiG-25 *Foxbat*,
fastest fighter of all. Below: the Lockheed YF-12A was
developed into the unarmed SR-71 Blackbird.

the type's maneuverability fully compensates for this. The Fighting Falcon can carry around 15,000 pounds of ordnance on short sorties, and has successfully replaced the F-104 Starfighter in the air forces of several European countries, where license-manufacturing deals have also been concluded.

The US Navy, too, could boast two potent new fighters that in many respects paralleled their USAF counterparts in role but were optimized for naval operation – the Grumman F-14 Tomcat and the McDonnell Douglas F-18 Hornet. The F-14 was tasked with long-range defense of the US Fleet when it entered service in 1972 as replacement for the still-born F-111B project. Its innovations included two particularly spectacular features in the automatic flight control system – which varies wing sweep during dogfighting without the aid of the pilot – and the Hughes AWG-9 radar. The latter was developed to match the F-14's six Hughes AIM-54 Phoenix air-to-air missiles originally intended for the F-111B, and can isolate individual aircraft in formation some 100 miles away before the missiles are assigned to down them. With a maximum speed of Mach 2.34, the Tomcat is a formidable addition to US Navy strength.

The F-18 Hornet was evolved from an unsuccessful Northrop-designed competitor in the lightweight fighter competition of 1974 that was won by the F-16 Fighting Falcon. It was adopted by McDonnell Douglas to fill a US Navy requirement for a low-cost multi-mission fighter; after modifications that included a considerable increase in fuel tankage to confer the required range, a new radar and structural strengthening to withstand catapult launch, the type finally reached operational status in the early Eighties. Two General Electric turbofans permit a maximum speed of Mach 1.8.

The role of the fighter in the Eighties is as much to obtain and maintain air superiority against its opponents than as interceptors of enemy bombers; surface-to-air missiles have largely taken over that task. Speed is not the only criterion to be considered; the Lockheed SR-71 Blackbird reconnaissance aircraft, for example, could rival the MiG-25 *Foxbat* in terms of speed, but – even if armed – could not dogfight at that speed. If *Foxbat* engaged in combat with Western warplanes at lower speeds and altitudes, its big advantage would be lost, and its reputed poor maneuverability and endurance would then count against it.

It seems likely, therefore, that Mach 3 or thereabouts will be the ceiling for manned fighters for some while to come – not only because of structural considerations but the limited applications of faster fighters. Any further developments may well take place outside the stratosphere – but in such oxygen-starved environments, rocket propulsion would be needed to augment turbojet power. Such 'aircraft' of the space age may provide interesting reading for the next generation.

**Above: four 1000-pound bombs transform this SEPECAT
Jaguar T.Mark 2 trainer into a potent attack aircraft.**

ATTACK

The first use of aircraft in wartime was as scouts – literally air observation platforms to observe troop movements. The logical development of this was for the aircraft to intervene directly in the course of the war on the ground. Vulnerability to ground fire was a major problem, while a degree of air superiority had to be maintained in order for the attacks to be pressed home successfully. The concept enjoyed a new lease of life in World War II, largely due to the success of the Junkers Ju 87 *Stuka* dive-bomber which, despite its low speed and poor defensive armament, proved deadly accurate when operating under cover of German fighter protection.

The Russian Ilyushin Il-2 Shturmovik was perhaps the most effective ground-attack aircraft of the war, while the US Navy's Dauntless, Helldiver and Avenger established a tradition for the service that would be continued in the jet age. At the cessation of hostilities, attack aircraft were once more put on the back burner to make way for fighter designs: Korea caught the majority of projected designs still on the drawing board or in flight testing. The Grumman F9F Panther was the ground-attack workhorse of the US Navy, while another straight-wing design, the Banshee, linked the name of McDonnell with naval aviation for what was to be a long and successful association.

One of the more advanced types to emerge in the post-Korea period was the Douglas A-3 Skywarrior. Rather larger and heavier than the Banshee and Panther, the prototype flew in 1952 and showed the type to be a pleasingly designed swept-wing bomber powered by two wing-mounted Westinghouse (later replaced by Pratt & Whitney J57) turbojets. With a crew of pilot, bombardier/co-pilot and navigator/gunner, the Skywarrior was able to deliver bombs from high or low levels at a speed of 610mph and at a range of up to 2900 miles.

Joining the fleet in 1957, the A-3 was the heaviest aircraft ever to have taken off from a carrier deck with a maximum weight of some 82,000 pounds – somewhat greater than that of a wartime B-17 Fortress. Its success can be gauged by the fact that no less than 18 US Navy units operated the type in the early Sixties. As the emphasis switched away from carrier-borne bombers to missile-armed submarines, however, the Navy successfully redeployed the Skywarrior as a flight refueling and/or electronic countermeasures aircraft, in which roles it served through Vietnam. A land-based variant, the B-66 Destroyer, served with the US Air Force in reconnaissance (RB), weather (WB) and electronic countermeasures (EB-66) versions.

With the US Navy's carrier-based aircraft now restricted to light strike duties, the Douglas A-4 Skyhawk quickly came into its own. Known as 'Heinemann's Hot Rod' after designer Ed Heinemann, the A-4 was small enough to fit onto an aircraft carrier lift without the necessity for cumbersome wing-folding

Left: the nimble Douglas A-4 Skyhawk, here shown in its two-seat TA-4J training version, served the US Navy with distinction from 1956. Above: rather larger than the Skyhawk but no less valuable as a carrier-based attack bomber was the Douglas A-3 Skywarrior.

apparatus – yet the diminutive jet packed a sizeable punch into that compact airframe. Production ran from 1954 to 1979, when the last of 2500 Skyhawks rolled off the production line. Like the British Hawker Hunter, another type with a high subsonic performance, it became a perennial favorite the world over, and numerous early marks were refurbished and updated for export sale when retired from US Navy service. Israel and Argentina were among the nations to show that the Skyhawk still presented a very real threat over two decades from its appearance, A-4s from the latter nation claiming the destroyer HMS *Coventry* during the Falklands conflict in 1982.

Two types to serve the US Navy in the electronic warfare and reconnaissance roles after being designed as purely attack types were the North American RA-5 Vigilante and the Grumman EA-6 Prowler. The Vigilante's Mach 2 capability was not enough to see it escape the fate of the Skywarrior when strategic shipboard strike aircraft were downgraded. Instead, its cavernous bomb-bay and a new under-fuselage fairing were packed with radar, sensors and cameras to transform the Vigilante into a significant and capable reconnaissance platform. Its aerodynamic qualities were recognized some six years later when the Mikoyan-Gurevich design bureau 'borrowed' the A-5's shoulder-mounted wing and distinctive engine air intakes in their Mach 3 *Foxbat* fighter.

The Grumman Intruder (named Prowler in its EA-6 variant) enjoyed a longer period of service as an attack aircraft. Designed to be able to press home its attack in any weather, the A-6 was fitted with DIANE (Digital Integrated Attack Navigational Equipment) and flew its first operational missions in early 1965 from the aircraft carrier USS *Independence* off Vietnam. Since then, the Intruder has been continually updated with anti-radiation missiles and ever more complex navigation aids and weapons systems. As the EA-6B Prowler (distinguishable by a longer nose section and a large fin-mounted fillet), the design received a new lease of life. A turbo generator in the nose powers the ten electronic jammers (mounted in four under-wing and one under-fuselage pod) that attempt to detect, analyze and ultimately render ineffective enemy radar. No armament is carried.

European shipborne attack aircraft became rapidly more advanced through the Fifties. The Hawker Sea Hawk provided the basis of the naval air arms of Britain, Holland, India and West Germany, but was a conventional straight-wing single-seater with a top speed of less than 600mph. Although the French Dassault Etendard, first flown in the Fifties, remained in the shadow of the Mirage family, its supersonic development the Super Etendard entered the Eighties in service with the French and Argentine navies. The type's integrated navigation/attack system enabled it to pose a significant threat to surface vessels.

The gradual reduction of the Royal Navy's carrier fleet in the Seventies left the service with only vertical take-off and helicopter types with which to face the next decade. In the case of the Hawker Siddeley Buccaneer, the Fleet Air Arm's loss was clearly the

Left: starting life as a shipborne attack type, the Hawker Siddeley Buccaneer later proved equally successful flying from land bases. Above: Sukhoi's Su-7 *Fitter* was a basic but popular Soviet fighter-bomber that serves with the Egyptian and other air forces.

Royal Air Force's gain, since the venerable two-seat strike aircraft (developed from the Blackburn NA39 of 1955) was to prove an effective and adaptable airframe – so much so that production restarted and newly-built Buccaneer S Mark 2B aircraft appeared in the RAF ranks alongside their ex-Navy forerunners. The T-tailed Buccaneer's toughened airframe, permitting high subsonic speeds at low level, together with the capability to accept improved systems and armaments, kept it in the front line for over two decades. Aside from its underwing hard-points, the type retained the rotating internal bomb-bay that facilitates weapons delivery at high speeds in the clean configuration – a rare capability indeed.

The transition from carriers to land bases was also made by the US Navy's Vought A-7 Corsair II, procured as a Skyhawk replacement by the US Navy. The type's swift progress from winning the design competition in 1964 to service delivery in 1966 was assisted by its derivation from a type already in US Navy service, the Vought F-8 Crusader fighter. The types differed in size (the A-7 was shorter), engine (the A-7 had a non-afterburning Allison/Rolls Royce turbofan as opposed to the F-8's Pratt & Whitney turbojet) and wing design, the A-7 foregoing the F-8's variable-incidence wing designed to keep the fuselage level at low speeds.

The US Air Force also purchased the A-7, and their land-based A-7D combined inertial navigation and attack systems with a 'head-up' display by which the pilot had the information projected into his line of vision.

The Soviet Union's main attack type of the Sixties was the Sukhoi Su-7. Known as *Fitter* to NATO, it was simply an old-fashioned fighter-bomber, using bombs, cannon and rockets to hit ground targets. Its supersonic top speed of Mach 1.6 was somewhat counterbalanced by its limited fuel capacity, with two large drag-inducing drop tanks being needed to attain even a 900-mile range. Although a basic type, the Su-7 proved an extremely popular export, seeing service with a dozen air arms in total, while a variable-geometry development, the Su-17 *Fitter-C* that entered service in the early Seventies, nearly doubled the ordnance load of its predecessor while carrying it up to 30 percent farther.

Another somewhat 'ordinary' fighter-bomber was one of the surprising successes of the Vietnam War. The Republic F-105 Thunderchief was nominally a Century Series fighter, being the last of those six designs to enter production. An all-weather-capable type, both the F-105D (the major production variant) and the two-seat F-105F struck repeatedly at enemy targets with 12,000 pounds of external stores as well as the contents of an internal bomb-bay. A number of F-105Fs were modified to accept electronic countermeasures equipment and carried Shrike anti-radiation missiles to strike surface-to-air missile sites in 'Wild Weasel' operations.

A flourishing sub-category of attack aircraft in the Sixties and Seventies was the low-cost COIN (counter-insurgency) type. Frequently employed by Third World countries for limited air-to-ground operations, these were light civilian or training aircraft that were converted to carry stores. Perceptive manufacturers from Europe and the US saw a ready market for designs that could double as training and attack aircraft, with ease of operation and simplicity of maintenance the most important factors. Aermacchi of Italy was an early arrival on the scene with the MB 326A, a type that found immediate favor with the air forces of Tunisia and Ghana. As the airframe was developed through sub-types G and L, it attracted large orders and a license-building agreement with EMBRAER of Brazil, who produced the MB 326 as the Xavante for the air arms of Brazil, Togo and Paraguay. The Xavante's armament loads were designed and manufactured in Brazil.

A single-seat development, the MB 326K, was flown in 1970 with improved load-carrying capacity, but had already been beaten into the air by the British Aerospace (BAC) Strikemaster. With its distinctive 'humped', pressurized single-seat cockpit, the type proved an amazingly effective redesign of the venerable 1958-vintage Jet Provost, the RAF's basic jet trainer. Powered by the same Rolls-Royce Viper turbojet used by the rival Macchi design, the Strikemaster created a record for repeat orders from satisfied export customers, serving with eight air arms and proving particularly popular in the Middle East. A truly prodigious range of armament on offer included ballistic, retarded or practice bombs, machine guns and rocket packs of various calibers. Meanwhile, the ideas developed by the Strikemaster design were used to provide the RAF with the pressurized Jet Provost T Mark 5, thereby extending the type's service life into a third decade.

As the name implies, COIN types concentrate on delivering maximum firepower at minimum cost and complexity of avionics and airframe, assuming that no concerted opposition will be encountered. In a European war, for example, no such assumption would hold, and a rather different philosophy was thus applied in the design of the Fairchild A-10 Thunderbolt II. This reversed the once-popular trend of employing obsolescent fighter types for ground attack, recognizing the need for maneuverability at low speeds and greater firepower to counteract the Warsaw Pact armor that had chillingly demonstrated its speed and effectiveness during the 1968 invasion of Czechoslovakia, accomplished in a single night.

The qualities that got the Thunderbolt the job included a bomb-load of up to 16,000 pounds, an ability to absorb punishment and survive, a short and rough-field capability and its relative economy when compared with the complex jet attack types it would replace. The A-10 was selected in preference to the rival (and considerably more conventional) Northrop A-9 in 1973. It is armed with one of the most impressive air-borne weapons ever, the General Electric GAU-8/A gun, the 30mm shells from which can penetrate any contemporary armor; this takes up most of the forward fuselage. The A-10's twin General Electric TF34 turbofans – the aircraft can get home on one – are mounted high on the rear fuselage, hidden by the wing from most ground fire, while the pilot and vital areas of the airframe are shielded by heavy titanium armor for maximum survivability. Most vital systems, including tail surfaces, are duplicated left and right.

With a maximum speed of only 518mph and no air-to-air combat capability whatsoever, the A-10 is clearly a specialized type that would require adequate air cover to be fully effective. Nevertheless it forms an important part of the US commitment to NATO, and effectively goes some way to neutralizing the Soviet advantages in armor over the West.

Above: the variety of bombs and rockets carried by this British Aerospace Strikemaster of the Sultan of Oman's Air Force attests to its effectiveness. Below: the EMBRAER Xavante was the Brazilian-built version of Macchi's MB326G counter-insurgency (COIN) type that could also fulfil a training role.

European designs placed a premium on short-field capability. The SEPECAT Jaguar, for example, can fly from a section of motorway or *autobahn* – something of an unexpected bonus from a Mach 1.6 tactical support type with a 10,500 pound weapons load. The type was developed from the mid-Sixties in collaboration between the British Aircraft Corporation (later British Aerospace) in Britain and Breguet in France, its two Adour turbofan engines also being the result of an Anglo-French partnership – this time between Rolls-Royce and Turbomeca. Jaguars of the Armee de l'Air were the first of the type to operate against ground forces when they were flown in Mauretania in 1978, while this attack capability won the Jaguar export orders from Oman, Ecuador and India.

Another successful multi-national design collaboration, on this occasion between Britain, Italy and West Germany, led to the Panavia Tornado. Originally designated MRCA (Multi-Role Combat Aircraft), the Tornado is a twin-engined, two seat variable-geometry type with great operating flexibility. Its two major versions are the IDS (Interdictor/Strike) and the ADV (Air Defence Variant), and it is the former that is used in the attack role, replacing such diverse types as the F-104G, Vulcan, Canberra and Buccaneer in West German, Italian and Royal Air Force service.

Its digital navigation and weapons-aiming system allow it to deliver some 18,000 pounds of stores (including air-to-surface missiles) with great accuracy, while a 'fly-by-wire' system, using electrical signals rather than the more usual mechanical linkages, saves weight. The Tornado can fly blind in all weathers and at any altitude, with automatic terrain-following enabling it to hug ground contours and fly in 'under the radar' without fear of detection. Unit cost of such a sophisticated type is obviously considerable, but the qualities already outlined – allied to a short-field capability conferred by its swing wing – make the Tornado an invaluable addition to the West's order of battle.

Although similar in configuration to the Tornado, the Soviet variable-geometry Mikoyan MiG-27 is more comparable to the Jaguar in terms of attack radius (575 miles) and payload (6600 pounds). It is the attack version of the MiG-23 *Flogger* interceptor fighter, and was introduced in 1975. Many simplifications were attempted to increase useful load, while fat tyres reflected Frontal Aviation's practice of operating for periods from temporary sites away from paved-runway airfields.

44

The Soviet response to the General Dynamics F-111 appeared in 1974 as the Sukhoi Su-24 *Fencer*, some 12 percent smaller but similar in layout to its US counterpart with side-by-side seating and two afterburning turbofans. Nearly twice as heavy as the MiG-27, alongside which it served in Soviet Frontal Aviation units in the Seventies, the Mach 2 Su-24 had the capability to reach most significant European targets from bases in East Germany. It was believed to register a five-fold increase in warload-range performance over the elderly Yak-28 *Brewer* it replaced.

A cloak of secrecy surrounded the type, and it was not allowed to fly outside Soviet airspace until mid-1979. US sources believe *Fencer* to have the capability to 'deliver ordnance in all weathers within 180

**Above: the vertical take-off British Aerospace Harrier.
Below: a Royal Navy Sea Harrier lands on deck.**

feet of its target', due to unusually sophisticated (by Soviet standards) terrain avoidance and navigation/attack systems.

An interesting collaborative venture in the attack field was initiated in the early Seventies by Yugoslavia and Romania; the result was the twin-turbojet IAR-93 Orao (Eagle), the design of which owed not a little to the Anglo-French Jaguar. Although prototypes powered by non-afterburning Rolls-Royce Viper turbojets had only subsonic performance, IAR-93B production aircraft were fitted with an afterburner that boosted performance to near-transonic levels. Further developments might well provide Warsaw Pact countries with a potent supersonic warplane that, unusually, owes nothing to Soviet design bureaux.

Perhaps the most remarkable attack aircraft in the world, the British Aerospace Harrier pioneered the vertical take-off and landing (VTOL) concept in operational service with the Royal Air Force. It was first flown as the Hawker P1127 in 1960, entering RAF service after a protracted development period in 1969. Thrust from the Harrier's Pegasus power plant not only exhausted rearward, as with conventional aircraft, but could also be vectored downwards by means of four nozzles to allow vertical take-off and landing on a cushion of air.

Since the Arab-Israeli war of 1967 highlighted the vulnerability of concrete runways to enemy attack, the Harrier's versatility has been much prized. It is operated usually in the STOVL (Short Take-Off/Vertical Landing) mission profile, since a greater offensive load can be carried if the Harrier employs a short take-off run. In shipboard service with the Royal Navy, it duplicated this by means of a 'ski-jump' ramp fitted to the bows of *Invincible* class cruisers. Sea Harriers also flew from the carrier HMS *Hermes* against Argentine forces in the Falklands campaign, but the type had earlier proved its mettle on land when four RAF Harriers were sent to the former Central American colony of Belize to back up ground forces in a sovereignty dispute.

McDonnell Douglas developed the type as the AV-8B, with a larger, super-critical wing and a greatly increased weapons load after standard versions of the Harrier had entered service with the US Marine Corps in 1971. The RAF also announced its intention to purchase substantial numbers of these to augment its German-based Harriers in the mid-Eighties – an ironic twist since a projected Mach 2 development, the P1154, had been cancelled some 20 years earlier and a chance to participate in the AV-8B program had been declined in the early Seventies. In US Marine Corps service, the Harrier doubles as an air combat fighter, a role it had not previously filled with the RAF, fitted with Sidewinder air-to-air missiles. The USMC pilots have developed the VIFF (Vectoring In Forward Flight) technique, which allows the type to turn on a sixpence or, indeed, a dime.

It was standard practise in the Seventies to include a ground attack capability in any specification for a new fighter. Most of the US Air Force's Seventies acquisitions could be pressed into service in this way, even when – as in the case of the F-16 – the fighter's prized maneuverability was sacrificed by the 'Christmas-tree effect' of hanging combinations of stores under the wing. In some cases, as with the MiG-27 development of the MiG-23, such attempts to make the fighter do double duty have resulted in the development of a specialized sub-type with maximized attack potential. This, together with the tank-busting A-10 and the cheaper jet trainer/attack types favored in the Third World, indicate that at long last the attack aircraft has carved its own niche in jet-age warfare.

BOMBERS

Since the only significant developments in jet bomber design to take place during World War II were terminated by the fall of the German Reich, the way was clear for the rule-books on bomber design to be rewritten as world peace approached. The jet engine offered not only the possibility of increased bomb-load, but also the opportunity to dispense with much of the cumbersome defensive armament that had made the Boeing B-17 Flying Fortress literally that. Now, it was reasoned, the jet-propelled bomber could evade interception and fulfil its mission without fear of aerial reprisal.

Despite such high hopes, the first jet bombers to appear inevitably took the form of compromise designs in which turbojets were substituted for piston engines (as with the Douglas XB-43 Mixmaster) or merely provided auxiliary power for a piston-powered type (the intercontinental-range Convair B-36, with four Pratt & Whitney J47 jets supplementing six radial engines). The first true jet bomber to see operational service was the North American B-45 Tornado, which was delivered to the US Air Force in late 1948 and was a conventional design similar to (but larger than) the company's piston-engined A-26 Invader.

Although the type saw service for around a decade, the four-engined B-45 betrayed its makers' reluctance to take the giant steps that would see airframe design catch up with the type's technologically advanced power plants. The Soviet Union's first production jet bomber, the Ilyushin Il-28 *Beagle*, first flew in late 1948 and was nearly as conservative in design.

Unlike the B-45, however, it featured swept flying surfaces in the vertical and horizontal tail, but its large tail turret and bulky fuselage owed much to the Tupolev Tu-4, an unlicensed copy of the US B-29 Superfortress. The tail gunner was one of the three crew members along with the pilot and bombardier – one less than the Tornado – while speed at 560mph was some 20mph inferior. The long-serving and durable Il-28 was widely exported to Communist satellites and Middle Eastern countries, while many hundreds were built in China. Power was provided by two license-built derivatives of the Rolls-Royce Nene turbojets given to the USSR by Britain after World War II.

Previous pages: a Boeing B-52G Stratofortress launches a cruise missile during trials. Left: the gigantic Convair B-36 used four podded jet engines to supplement its radial power plants. Below: another design to feature propeller and jet engines was the Douglas XB-42A; the similar XB-43 Mixmaster flew on turbojet power alone.

Above: unusual in featuring swept tail surfaces and a
forward-swept trailing edge to the wing, the Ilyushin
Il-28 *Beagle* was a conventional design in all other
respects. It was widely used by Soviet bloc countries and
client nations such as Egypt, in whose colors it is pictured.

CANBERRA T·17
ROLE   Electronic counter measures
        training
ENGINES   2 Avon Mk 1
           6500lb static thrust
NUMBER BUILT   24 (Converted B2)
SQUADRON EQUIPPED   360

Left: a versatile performer, the English Electric
Canberra served with the Indian Air Force in its photo-
reconnaissance PR. Mark 57 version. Below: a fine view
of the B. Mark 6 bomber in Royal Air Force service.
Below left: among the many tasks for which the Canberra
was modified was electronic countermeasures training, a
T. Mark 17 being illustrated. Bottom left: the Glenn L.
Martin Company built the type as the B-57 for the US
Air Force.

Rolls-Royce engines also powered the similarly-
configured English Electric Canberra, which first
flew in May 1949 and joined its US and Soviet contemporaries in front-line service in 1951. Like the
Il-28, it was to prove long-serving, refurbished ex-
RAF examples continuing to fly with several Third
World air arms in the Eighties. Back in the Fifties,
however, its roles included bombing, photo-recon-
naissance and training, and as such it was able to
supplant several different piston-engined types in the
RAF order of battle. A Canberra became the first jet
to fly the Atlantic without refueling *en route* when one
of two aircraft delivered to the Glenn L. Martin
Company in the United States crossed in a time of 4
hours 40 minutes in February 1951. The type subse-
quently became one of the few British-designed aircraft to enter service in quantity with the US Air
Force; Martin flew their US-built B-57 version in
1954 and developed it to become a sophisticated
tactical bomber and reconnaissance type that served
in Vietnam.

The strategic bomber had been one of the success
stories of World War II. The Allied bombing offensive against the German cities had proved shattering
to enemy morale, while the great range of the Boeing
B-29 Superfortress had enabled it to deliver the
nuclear strikes that had foreshortened the war in the
East. To maintain its status as a world power, the US

needed to find a jet equivalent to the Superfort, and
its first steps were taken as early as 1947 with the
maiden flight of the Boeing B-47 Stratojet. Six
General Electric J47 turbojets were podded singly
and in pairs, slung forward on pylons from the knife-
edge shoulder wing and augmented on take-off by 18
fuselage-mounted rocket motors. With its 35 degrees
of wing sweep, tandem outrigger undercarriage and
futuristic design, the Stratojet seemed an age apart
from the lumbering B-36 then leading the USAF's
front-line bomber force of piston-engined types.
Although the types' bomb-loads were hardly comparable – the production B-47 carried 22,000 pounds
as opposed to the B-36's 72,000 pounds – the writing
was clearly on the wall for the piston-engined bomber.
The Stratojet served into the Seventies in specially-
converted versions, but it was its larger stablemate,
the B-52 Stratofortress, that was to prove a more
formidable marriage of jet-age design and maximum
bomb-load.

As manufacturers of the UK's prime heavy bombers
of World War II in the Halifax and Lancaster respectively, the firms of Handley Page and Avro were more
than interested in supplying the RAF with their jet
counterparts. Each selected a different and intriguing
answer to the problem of producing a high-speed
(though subsonic) jet bomber capable of delivering a
bomb-load in excess of 25,000 pounds. The Ministry

Above: the unusual crescent-wing planform of the
Handley Page Victor is shown to effect in this aerial view
from a sister aircraft. Below: like the Victor, the Hawker
Siddeley Vulcan was intended for high-level operations
and initially bore a white anti-flash finish. This Vulcan
B. Mark 2 carries two US-built Skybolt stand-off missiles.

of Defence showed a remarkable lack of faith in the two firms, commissioning a third, Vickers, to build a conventional alternative in the Valiant and ending up with three directly comparable yet different aircraft in their V-force. The Handley Page Victor employed a crescent-wing planform that claimed to give excellent handling at all speeds, while the large, predatory-looking delta of the Avro Vulcan immediately made it one of the world's most distinctive aircraft.

The Valiant was first to enter service but was found to suffer metal fatigue and retired prematurely in the mid-Sixties. Finding themselves with a surfeit of V-bombers, the RAF had converted a number of Valiants into flight refueling tankers, and this modi-

fication was later applied with greater success to the Victor, which served on into the Eighties in this role, and finally the Vulcan. When the Vulcan and Victor entered service in 1957 and 1958 respectively, their major weapon was the Blue Steel stand-off missile, to be delivered from altitude. The white anti-flash finish adapted for this role was to give way to camouflage, however, when they were pressed into service at lower levels in later years.

The fact that the V-bombers were to stand alone as the mainstays of the RAF's bomber force in the Sixties and most of the Seventies could not have been contemplated at the time of their design: nevertheless, they proved surprisingly adaptable. Like the Americans, the RAF had switched its bombers to low-level

operations in the mid-Sixties as the manned bomber's vulnerability to radar detection and SAM attack became apparent. The Vulcan bore the brunt of the redefinition of roles, being operated as a low-level conventional bomber, and in 1982, on the brink of retirement, was called upon to operate in earnest for the first time against the Argentine garrison on the Falkland Island capital of Port Stanley. Ironically, its deployment was facilitated by in-flight refueling from its sister Victors. The Valiant had been the only other V-bomber previously to have seen action, in Suez in 1956.

Left: a turboprop Tupolev Tu-95 *Bear* meets US Phantoms.

Above: Myashishchev's M-4 *Bison* in Soviet naval service.

The Soviet response to Western strategic bomber designs was in many ways conventional. The long, slim fuselage shape owed much to the Tu-4 Super-fortress copy, as indeed did all their Forties and Fifties bomber designs. The wing was swept back, Stratojet-style, in modern fashion, reflecting contemporary thought on wing planforms. Yet the totally unexpected feature of the Tupolev Tu-95 *Bear* was the fact that it had propellers. Realizing that their current technology could not create an innova-tive bomber design, they opted for the long range and an endurance of over 24 hours conferred by the *Bear*'s four turboprops over pure speed. Even so, the *Bear* could outpace most of the straight-winged jet fighters that opposed it on its entry to service in 1955, but the advantage was to be shortlived. As the Sixties approached, the Tu-95 adopted the mighty AS-3 *Kangaroo* air to surface missile to counter its vulnera-bility to the new breed of all-weather fighters entering service; as the *Bear-B* weapons platform, it could loiter at will outside their range while still posing a significant threat.

One of the most unusually-configured warplanes of the postwar era with its combination of swept wing and contra-rotating turboprops, the Tu-95 remained in the Soviet order of battle into the mid-Eighties. Although long obsolete as a bomber, the *Bear-D* was a frequent visitor to the fringes of Western airspace operating in an intelligence-gathering role, for which it was crammed with electronic equipment and a large ventral radar radome, possibly for surface-to-surface missile direction. With its range of 11,000 miles and phenomenal endurance, the *Bear* was literally irreplaceable, although vibrations from the turboprop engines must have necessitated much re-structuring work to maintain the numbers required for front-line service.

Despite pinning their faith in the fuel-conscious turboprop, the Soviet Union did back the *Bear* with two pure jet types in the Fifties – the Tupolev Tu-16 and the Myashishchev M-4 *Bison*. *Badger*, as the Tu-16 was known, first flew in 1952 and was a type roughly comparable in configuration and size to the American Stratojet. Although only a twin-engined type, the Tu-16 was built around the extremely powerful Mikulin AM-3 turbojet, each of which developed no less than 18,000 pounds thrust and enabled *Badger* to boast an impressive bomb-load of some 13,000 pounds. More often carried, however, were examples of the Soviet range of air-to-surface missiles, and it was in the missile-carrying role that the Tu-16 served successfully through the Sixties with AVMF, the Soviet naval air arm.

Much larger but somewhat less successful was the Myashishchev M-4 *Bison*, initially powered by four of the *Badger*'s Mikulin AM-3 power plants but later re-engined with more powerful Sovloviev units. Although a pre-production version designated 201M established speed records in 1959, the type's range and ceiling were disappointing and, as its low-slung outrigger undercarriage layout precluded the use of ASMs due to inadequate ground clearance, it was to survive mainly as a tanker and reconnaissance plat-form in the Seventies, in much the same way as the RAF's Victor to which it was a counterpart. Like *Bear* and *Badger*, *Bison* was subject to constant updating of airframe and equipment during its service life.

The Boeing B-52 Stratofortress took the company's tradition for building the world's largest and most impressive bombers to its ultimate conclusion. A massive, multi-wheeled leviathan, its giant 185-foot wing drooped alarmingly on the tarmac, supported only by outrigger wheels near the tips. No fewer than eight Pratt & Whitney J57 engines propelled the

Stratofortress skyward with a bomb-load of up to 60,000 pounds, some 12 times that of the World War II Fortress. The formation of the US (Army) Air Force's Strategic Air Command in 1946 signified an intention to possess a world-girdling strategic strike force, and the B-52 was its chosen weapon and flagship.

The type's baptism of fire was in Vietnam in 1965 – three years after the production lines at Boeing's Wichita plant had shut down and ten years after its introduction to service. In contrast to the final production marks which carried stand-off weapons and decoy missiles, enabling them to hit three separate targets, the first aircraft to see active service were B-52Ds converted to carry 85 500-pound 'iron' bombs. Switched from supply-route strikes in South Vietnam to operations against the North in 1966, the Stratofortress kept up a fearsome bombardment into the Seventies – but with the advanced SAM types in the North Vietnamese armory it had become apparent that bombing operations with the B-52 over enemy territory involved an unacceptable risk. So, like the Vulcan and Victor, it donned camouflage and was flown at low altitude for the duration. Despite such harsh treatment, a billion-dollar program of refurbishment and re-manufacture was undertaken and the Stratofortress seems likely to remain on USAF strength for the rest of the century.

With the superpowers becalmed in the mid-Sixties, France made a dramatic entry into the strategic bomber field with the Dassault Mirage IV. Developed from the Mirage fighter family, the mark combined Mach 2 performance with the capability of delivering a 60 kiloton nuclear free-fall bomb carried semi-recessed in the fuselage. With a modest tactical radius of 770 miles considerably augmented by the French fleet of Boeing C-135F in-flight refueling tankers, the two-seat delta-wing type was dispersed in shelters ready for immediate action. The Mirage IV was due to be retired in the mid-Eighties after two decades of service in favor of silo-based missiles, but had undoubtedly proved its worth long since.

Following the introduction of the B-52 and its contemporaries a lull in bomber design ensued – mainly as a result of the diversion of world attention toward the missile stockpiles being amassed by the superpowers. The existence of the Intercontinental Ballistic Missile (ICBM) caused all previous assumptions about the necessity for manned aircraft to come under scrutiny, and several promising projects were inevitably to perish in this climate of uncertainty. One such casualty was the BAC TSR-2, a two-seat shoulder-wing bomber, designed as a 'supersonic Canberra', which could deliver a similar bomb-load from high or low altitudes and escape at speeds of up to Mach 2.5. Prototypes were ordered and flown in 1964, but the program was cancelled shortly afterwards.

Above: the two AGM-28 Hound Dog missiles carried by the B-52G variant of the Boeing Stratofortress combined with the type's internal bomb-load to permit three separate targets to be attacked. The missiles' jet engines could be used to assist take-off.

59

Below: a B-52 refuels from a Boeing KC-135 Stratotanker.
Bottom: the BAC TSR-2 was a promising British
supersonic bomber that failed to reach production.

Above: the undisclosed range and performance of Tupolev's variable-geometry Tu-26 *Backfire* bomber caused the US considerable problems during strategic arms limitation negotiations.

The Soviets were first among the superpowers to wake to the continuing need for a strategic jet bomber in their inventory and answered it in dramatic style with the Tu-26. Code-named *Backfire*, it introduced a variable-geometry wing and Kuznetsov turbofan engines. These offered flexibility and economy, with a long subsonic range a possible alternative to supersonic dash to the target.

Backfire was Tupolev's follow-up to the Tu-22 *Blinder* fixed-wing bomber that had appeared in the mid-Sixties; indeed, *Backfire* is sometimes known as the Tu-22M. Despite the similarity in designation, the aircraft were completely different. *Blinder* was a contemporary of the Convair B-58 Hustler and had been intended to replace the Tu-16 *Badger*, but its supersonic top speed was insufficient to beat Western fighter defenses.

Despite *Backfire*'s suspected potency, its capabilities were officially minimized by the Soviet authorities for political reasons. The US authorities considered it a strategic bomber and thus limited by the SALT (strategic arms limitation) dialogue that continued between the powers, while its makers contended that, although the Tu-26 could strike at targets on the US mainland, it lacked the necessary reserves of fuel to complete the round trip. Sources suggest that drag caused by the wheel-well fairings protruding from the wing trailing edge of early versions similar to those of the Tu-22 *Blinder* restricted the planned range of 9500 miles. The *Backfire-B* development eliminated these, but range was still reckoned to be no more than that of the earlier Myashishchev M-4. It is now accepted that *Backfire* presents its major threat to Europe and China, unless used as a platform for launching cruise missiles.

As furious debate ensued as to *Backfire*'s classification as a strategic (intercontinental) or tactical type,

Below: France's Dassault Mirage IV provides that nation's Armée de L'Air with a surprisingly effective strategic bomber that allies a Mach 2 top speed with the ability to deliver a nuclear weapon.

Above: production of the Rockwell B-1B supersonic bomber in the eighties followed extensive flight trials and considerable political opposition. Overleaf: An FB-111A with SRAM.

the US development of its own manned bomber for the Eighties was undergoing a torrid flight to operational service – hindered not by development problems but political opposition. The Rockwell B-1 was rather larger than the *Backfire*, despite sharing its swing-wing planform, and allied a range of 7450 miles with an impressive maximum speed for its size of over Mach 1.2. The project was cancelled in 1977 by the Carter administration, but reinstated in modified form as the multi-role B-1B by President Reagan. It was now considered to provide not only a conventional bombing capability, but also a platform for cruise missiles to serve alongside submarine and land-launched missiles as one corner of the so-called 'Triad' defense system. The moveable bulkhead in the B-1B's forward bomb-bay reflects the fact that the cruise missile it carries was developed for delivery by the larger B-52, but its radar 'signature' is less than one percent of that of its predecessor. It will be able to carry out the B-52's aerial minelaying and surveillance

roles, as well as anti-submarine patrols. It is reckoned that the B-1B will be able to penetrate any predicted Soviet defenses until the 1990s with its computer-operated defensive avionics, and operate in less heavily-defended areas into the next century.

The future of the manned bomber in the Eighties seemed a little more assured than in the previous decade, with both superpowers retaining it as offering a more flexible option than missiles alone despite its relative expense and vulnerability. Already, the next Soviet bomber generation has been heralded by reports of the variable-geometry Tupolev *Blackjack*, some 20 percent larger than the B-1B and 40 percent larger than *Backfire*. With a maximum speed in excess of Mach 2 and a range of over 8000 miles, it is likely to enter service in 1986. So the pendulum continues to swing between East and West in a battle of wits and wills that should see the bomber survive in one form or another into the Twenty-First Century – hopefully without dropping a bomb in anger.

Index

Acknowledgments
Photographs are from the
collection of the author, Michael
J H Taylor with the following
exceptions:
Air BP 8 (top)
British Aerospace/Paul Cullerne
    15 (top)
Denis Hughes 11 (top), 26, 39, 42/3
RAF Museum, Hendon 20/1
Bob Snyder 23